Contents

KU-015-477

Welcome to the show 4

The world of dogs 6

Ancient breeds 8

Bred for speed 10

The Ultimate Pony Show 12

The world of cats 14

How do genes work? 16

Puppies and kittens 18

Best in Show 20

Brother and sister 22

The odd puppy out 24

Champion sniffers 26

The world's best-trained dog 28

Glossary 30

Find out more 31

Index 32

Some words are shown in bold, **like this**. You can find out what they mean by looking in the glossary.

Welcome to the show

Welcome to the Ultimate Pet Show – the world's best and biggest pet show. Here you can see pets of every kind, from pigeons to ponies. You plan to visit the dog, cat, and pony shows. On the way, you hope to find out about animal breeding and how **inheritance** works.

Breeds and traits

Your first stop is the Ultimate Dog Show. Over a hundred **breeds** of dogs are on display here. A breed is a distinct type of dog with certain **traits** or features. For example, a Dalmatian has long legs, short hair, and a spotty coat. Over many years, these features have been developed through breeding.

At a dog show, thousands of dogs compete to win the top prize of Best in Show.

Inheritance of Traits

Why Is My Dog Bigger Than Your Dog?

Jen Green

a Capstone company — publishers for children

Raintree is an imprint of Capstone Global Library Limited, a company incorporated in England and Wales having its registered office at 7 Pilgrim Street, London, EC4V 6LB – Registered company number: 6695582

www.raintreepublishers.co.uk
myorders@raintreepublishers.co.uk

Text © Capstone Global Library Limited 2014
First published in hardback in 2014
Paperback edition first published in 2015
The moral rights of the proprietor have been asserted.

Edited by Adam Miller, Sian Smith and Penny West
Designed by Philippa Jenkins
Original illustrations © Capstone Global Library Ltd 2014
Illustrated by Medi-mation
Picture research by Tracy Cummins
Originated by Capstone Global Library Ltd
Produced by Victoria Fitzgerald
Printed and bound in China by CTPS

ISBN 978 1 406 27427 1 (hardback)
17 16 15 14 13
10 9 8 7 6 5 4 3 2 1

ISBN 978 1 406 27434 9 (paperback)
18 17 16 15 14
10 9 8 7 6 5 4 3 2 1

Green, Jen
Inheritance of Traits: Why Is My Dog Bigger Than Your Dog? (Show Me Science)
A full catalogue record for this book is available from the British Library.

Acknowledgements
We would like to thank the following for permission to reproduce photographs:
Corbis p. 5 (© Ocean); Getty Images pp. 4 (New York Daily News Archive), 10 (John Mechalas), 11 (Abraham Cooper), 19 (Jane Burton), 20 (Joe Kohen), 26 (PAUL J. RICHARDS), 28 (Alexey Sokolov); Photo Researchers pp. 18 (Brian Evans), 23 (Addenbrookes Hospital / Science Source), 24 (William H. Mullins / Science Source); Shutterstock pp. 6 (© Artem Kursin), 8 (© ventdusud), 9 (© Pichugin Dmitry), 13 (© Cheryl Ann Quigley), 14 (© Anton Gvozdikov), 22 (© Linn Currie); Superstock pp. 7 (Biosphoto), 12 (Amiel / Photocuisine), 15 (Juniors), 16 (Juniors), 27 (Animals Animals).

Cover photograph of a Papillon and a Great Dane reproduced with permission of Corbis (© Don Mason).

We would like to thank Michael Bright for his invaluable help in the preparation of this book.
Every effort has been made to contact copyright holders of material reproduced in this book. Any omissions will be rectified in subsequent printings if notice is given to the publishers.

Disclaimer
All the Internet addresses (URLs) given in this book were valid at the time of going to press. However, due to the dynamic nature of the Internet, some addresses may have changed, or sites may have changed or ceased to exist since publication. While the author and publishers regret any inconvenience this may cause readers, no responsibility for any such changes can be accepted by either the author or the publishers.

Genes are the reason that young animals, like this Basset Hound, look like their parents.

Genes and inheritance

Dogs, cats, ponies, and all living things pass on features to their **offspring**. This process is called inheritance or **heredity**. Inheritance happens because of tiny structures called **genes**. Genes control features such as the length and colour of a dog's hair. Genes are the reason dogs give birth to puppies and cats give birth to kittens, not the other way around!

What are genes?

Genes are found inside **cells** – the tiny units that make up an animal's body. When animals reproduce (have young), genes work like a masterplan or blueprint. They form a set of instructions that control how the babies develop.

The world of dogs

At the Ultimate Dog Show, you can see dogs of all sizes. There are huge Great Danes, chunky Saint Bernards, and tiny Chihuahuas. A big, heavy Saint Bernard may weigh a hundred times more than a Chihuahua!

Same but different

As you wander around, you notice that dogs vary in shape as well as size. For example, Afghan Hounds are tall and long-legged, with long noses and long, silky fur. Pugs are small and stocky, with snubbed noses and short fur. Despite these differences, all dogs belong to the same **species** – the **domestic** dog.

This Chihuahua is many times smaller than this Mastiff.

LITTLE AND LARGE

Great Danes and Irish Wolfhounds are the tallest dogs, standing up to 1 metre (39 inches) at the shoulder. Saint Bernards are the heaviest dogs, weighing up to 90 kilograms (200 pounds). At the other end of the scale, the tiny Chihuahua stands only 20 centimetres (8 inches) tall, and may weigh just 1 kilogram (2 pounds).

Different jobs

Different **breeds** of dog have been developed to do different work. Border Collies were bred to herd sheep. Gun dogs, such as Labradors, were developed to fetch animals shot by hunters. Hounds, with their excellent sense of smell, were bred to track prey such as deer. Fierce-looking mastiffs were developed as guard dogs. Small or "toy" dogs were originally bred as hot water bottles, to keep their owners warm!

Dachshunds come in long-haired, wire-haired, and smooth-haired varieties.

You reach an area where some of the world's oldest dog **breeds** are on show. You stop to look at a Siberian Husky. These dogs were developed many centuries ago to pull sledges in the Arctic. With its thick fur and powerful build, the Siberian Husky looks a lot like the **ancestor** of all dogs, the wolf.

How did dogs develop?

You stop by a display screen that explains the connection between dogs and wolves. It says **domestic** dogs have been around for at least 12,000 years. The ancestors of modern dogs were probably young, hungry wolves that entered hunters' camps in search of food. The hunters tamed the animals and discovered they could be used to help with hunting or to guard the camp.

Siberian Huskies, shown here, and Alsatians (German Shepherds) look similar to wolves.

Cave paintings like this one from North Africa show that dogs have helped humans for thousands of years.

Over the next few thousand years, domestic dogs developed. But all these dogs were not alike. Some were fast and good at tracking. Others were fierce and made good guard dogs. Others were small and cuddly. All the breeds of dog that we know today developed from these beginnings.

The dog family

Wolves and domestic dogs are members of the family of dog-like animals called canines. Jackals and wild dogs belong to the same family. Foxes are also related. All canines are meat-eating hunters, with strong legs and sharp teeth to outrun and kill their prey.

You reach a section where Greyhounds are on show. You study a Greyhound's lean, muscular body and watch a video about Greyhound racing, which shows the dogs speeding around a racetrack. With its long head and neck, flexible body, and powerful legs, every part of a Greyhound's body is built for speed.

Selective breeding

The Greyhound **breed** was developed over many years through a process called **selective breeding**. Breeders selected (chose) their very fastest, strongest animals to breed from. Over time, the breed became even stronger and faster, with animals reaching record speeds. Modern Greyhounds can run at up to 72 kilometres (45 miles) per hour over a short distance.

Greyhounds are born with a natural instinct and ability to run.

Born to run

Greyhounds are an ancient breed. These dogs were developed over 4,000 years ago to hunt antelope. Later they were bred for track racing.

This picture of two Greyhounds was painted in 1812.

For centuries, breeders selected animals without understanding how **inheritance** worked. Now we know that features pass from parents to their young through **genes**, which are found inside **cells**. In the late 1800s, the development of powerful microscopes allowed scientists to see inside cells for the first time. This was a big step towards the discovery of genes.

The Ultimate Pony Show

You fancy a break from the dog show and head off to the Ultimate Pony Show. The show includes horses of different sizes, from large, heavy draught horses to small Shetland ponies. Their coats vary in colour from black to chestnut, grey, white, and golden. Some horses have spotty or piebald (patchy) markings.

Taming wild horses

There are over a hundred horse **breeds**, all descended from wild horses that galloped over the plains of Asia about 6,000 years ago. As horses were tamed, people noticed that they could be useful in many ways. They could carry soldiers into battle and pull carts or chariots.

In some parts of the world, horses are still used to pull farm equipment.

Developing horse breeds

Over time, different breeds of horses were developed to do different jobs. Some were bred to carry riders. Others were bred to pull coaches and carriages. Draught horses were developed to haul ploughs and other farm equipment. A farmer breeding draught horses would select his biggest and strongest horses to breed from. A breeder might also **mate** a strong horse with a fast one, to get a foal (baby horse) with both speed and strength.

The variety of horses

The smallest pony is the Falabella, which stands just 75 centimetres (30 inches) tall at the shoulder. The largest draught horses stand over 180 centimetres (70 inches) tall and weigh over 1,000 kilograms (2,200 pounds).

The World of Cats

The Ultimate Cat Show is in the next hall. You marvel at the variety of **breeds** on show. All **domestic** cats are descended from tabby-coloured African wildcats. Cats were kept as pets in ancient Egypt over 3,500 years ago. They helped Egyptian farmers by killing rats and mice.

A variety of cats

Looking around, you see that cats vary in shape and colour, just as dogs and horses do. You stop to admire a Persian, with its long, fluffy fur and flattish face. Not far away, Siamese cats are on show. They have short fur and longer noses. There are cats with long, fluffy tails, short tails, and Manx cats with no tails at all!

Cats vary in colour from black to grey, white, fawn, ginger, and tabby.

THE CAT FAMILY

The domestic cat belongs to the cat family, which has 37 **species**. The family is divided into big cats and small cats. Big cats include the lion, tiger, and leopard. Ocelots, servals, and wildcats are small cats.

Natural skills and instincts

Whether large or small, all cats have similar body shapes. They also share certain instincts and abilities. All cats are strong, agile, and good at climbing. They have keen senses, especially sight. All cats are meat-eating hunters. Hunting is a natural instinct, even in pet cats. All these qualities pass from parents to their young through **genes**.

The cat's natural hunting ability is used by farmers to control mice.

How do genes work?

You stop by a breeder who is showing two prize-winning cats – a male and a female. A sign says either animal can be hired for breeding. You talk to the breeder, who explains about **inheritance** and **genes**.

This prize-winning cat is a Maine Coon **breed**.

CAT SHOW WINNER

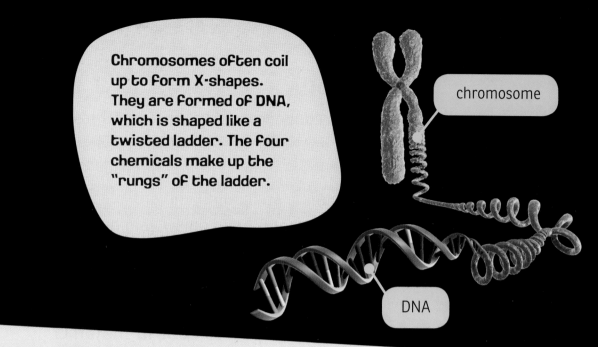

Chromosomes often coil up to form X-shapes. They are formed of DNA, which is shaped like a twisted ladder. The four chemicals make up the "rungs" of the ladder.

chromosome

DNA

All about genes

Genes are found in the **cell nucleus** – the tiny blob that acts as the cell's control centre. Genes are sections of long strands called **chromosomes**. Each chromosome carries thousands of genes. Each gene is like a small snippet of information, carrying the instructions for a particular feature, such as fur colour. The full set of instructions works like a blueprint to build new baby animals, such as puppies, kittens, and foals.

Genes are made of chemicals called **DNA**. DNA has four special chemicals that are arranged in different ways. Just as the letters of the alphabet can be arranged to spell words, so the arrangement of the chemicals forms a code. The code tells cells how to work and develop.

NUMBERS OF CHROMOSOMES

Different types of animals have different numbers of chromosomes in their cells. Cats have 38 chromosomes, dogs have 78, and horses have 64. Humans have 46 chromosomes. The actual number is not very important, but the number is always even because chromosomes come in pairs.

Puppies and kittens

You head back towards the dog show. On your way, you pass a pen with a female cat and her litter of kittens. Nearby is a display that explains how animals reproduce (have young).

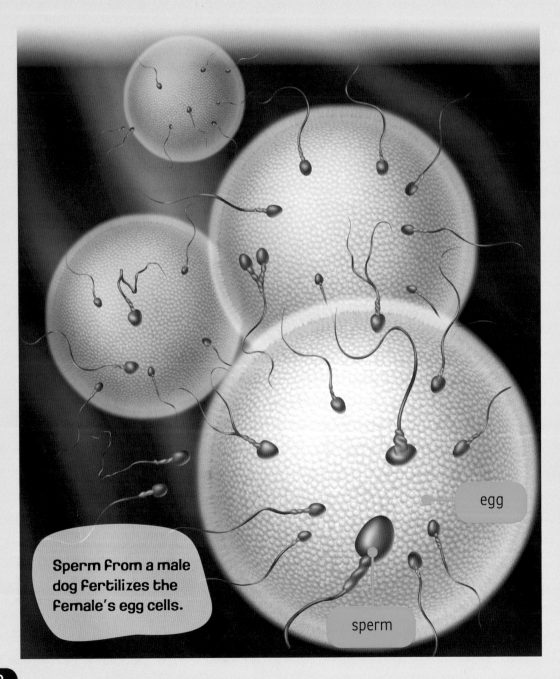

Sperm from a male dog fertilizes the female's egg cells.

egg

sperm

New life

Dogs, cats, and horses are **mammals**. Humans are also mammals. In all mammals, reproduction begins when a male **mates** with a female. New life starts when a sex **cell** from the male, called **sperm**, joins with the female's egg cell. This moment is called **fertilization**. In all mammals, fertilization happens inside the mother. The baby develops in a space called the **womb**.

The fertilized cell divides many times to form a ball of cells that slowly develops into a baby. As more cells are made, **genes** instruct the cells to develop into different types, which eventually form different body parts. When the baby is fully developed, it is born.

Gestation and litter sizes

Mammals give birth to different numbers of young. In each case, the babies spend a certain time developing inside the mother. This time is called **gestation**. Both dogs and cats give birth after about 9 weeks. A female dog may have between 1 and 12 puppies, while a cat may have up to 10 kittens. Foals spend 11 months in gestation. Usually only one foal is born, but sometimes there are twins.

Back at the dog show, some classes have been judged. A Beagle wins first prize. Show dogs often have long, odd-sounding names. The winner's name is Sophie III Amazing Trick of Hounslow. Her owners call her Trixie for short!

A full set of genes

You talk to the breeder, who explains that Trixie was bred from two prize-winning dogs. Their names were Clever Trick of Hounslow and Sophie II Amazing Lady. Trixie's full name reflects her parentage, but the breeder explains that she got more than her name from her parents. She also inherited half her **genes** from her mother and half from her father.

First steps

Some newborn **mammals** are more helpless than others. Newborn puppies and kittens are weak and cannot stand. Their eyes are closed, so they cannot see. Within two weeks their eyes open and they start to crawl about. Foals are able to stand on their long, wobbly legs just an hour after birth. After a few hours, they can run!

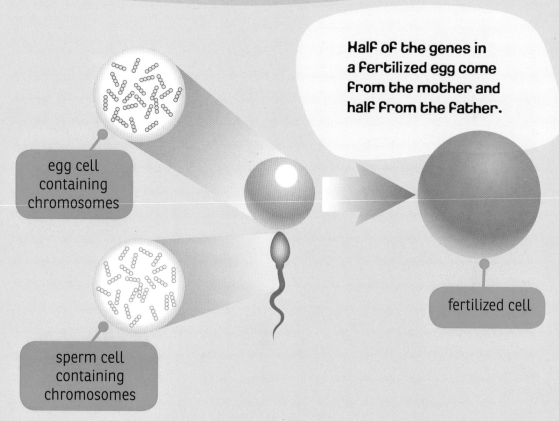

Half of the genes in a fertilized egg come from the mother and half from the father.

egg cell containing chromosomes

sperm cell containing chromosomes

fertilized cell

How does this **inheritance** happen? Well, you remember that dogs have 78 **chromosomes** in almost all of their **cells**. However, sex cells (**sperm** and egg) are different. They only contain half the normal number of chromosomes – 39 chromosomes in dogs. When the sperm joins with the egg, it forms the full set of 78 chromosomes that are needed to build a puppy like Trixie.

Brother and sister

The breeder is also showing a brother and sister pair, called Reggie and Ellie. You notice that brother and sister look similar, but their faces and markings are slightly different. If the two dogs come from the same litter, and inherited half their **genes** from each parent, why don't they look exactly the same?

These prize-winning dogs are related, but have different markings.

Variation

For centuries, breeders have known that within each **generation** of young that is born, some animals are slightly different. For example, one puppy might have slightly longer ears than normal. These differences, called **variations**, happen naturally. If breeders like the variation, they choose that animal to breed from. In this way, the feature becomes more common. Variation allows **breeds** to change over time.

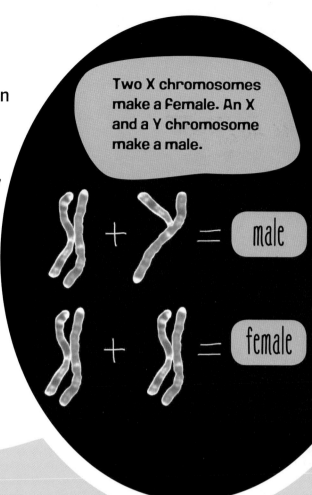

Two X chromosomes make a female. An X and a Y chromosome make a male.

male

female

Changing places

Puppies in a litter have similar, but not identical, genes. This is because when sex **cells** are made, some of the genes change places. Each **sperm** cell and each egg cell contains a different selection of genes. When the sex cells join, there is a different combination every time.

Boy or girl?

What makes some puppies male and others female? This is decided by a pair of **chromosomes** called sex chromosomes. The mother's egg always has an X chromosome, half the code for a female. The father's sperm may contain an X or a Y chromosome. If the sperm adds another X, the puppy will be female. If it adds a Y, the puppy will be male.

The odd puppy out

You stop by a pen that holds a black Labrador with her litter of four puppies. The proud father, another black Labrador, is nearby. But wait! You notice that one of the puppies is brown! How can two black dogs produce a brown puppy?

Genes have decided the colour of these puppies.

Strong and weak genes

You ask the owner, who reminds you that **genes** come in pairs. One of the pair comes from each parent, but both control the same feature, such as hair colour. In Labradors, the gene for black hair is stronger than the gene for brown hair. We call the strong gene **dominant** and the weak gene **recessive**. If one dog passes on the black-hair gene and the other passes on the brown-hair gene, the puppy will be black.

If two black dogs with one black-hair gene and one brown-hair gene **mate** and have several puppies, the chances are that one puppy will be brown. This puppy has received the brown-hair gene from both the father's **sperm** and the mother's egg.

Gregor Mendel

In the 1860s, Austrian scientist Gregor Mendel experimented with **heredity** by breeding pea plants. Mendel crossed plants producing violet flowers with ones producing white flowers and got only plants with violet flowers. However, when he bred the new violet-flowered plants together, he got some plants that produced white flowers. He realized that the violet flower colour was strong and the white flower colour was weak. It was not until many years later that scientists discovered the colours were controlled by strong and weak genes.

Champion sniffers

You head across to the central show ring to watch a display of sniffer dogs. These dogs are trained to use their excellent sense of smell. They are used in police work to sniff out explosives, track criminals by scent, and find people lost in the wild.

This Beagle is a trained sniffer dog.

Training and performance

You watch as a dog sniffs out a hidden package. The dog has inherited its excellent sense of smell and the instinct to sniff things out. But years of training have increased its tracking skills. Training has also strengthened the bond between the dog and its owner, so it is able to obey different commands and carry out a range of tasks.

A Bloodhound's nose is a thousand times more sensitive than a human's.

Genes play a big part in any dog's appearance. For example, they determine its size and the shapes of its body parts, such as its legs, ears, nose, and tail. However, diet and exercise also affect how a dog looks. Dogs that are given too much food can become overweight. Not enough food makes a dog thin. Exercise increases a dog's stamina (staying power) and strengthens its muscles, so it can run for longer without getting tired.

The work of sniffer dogs

Sniffer dogs are trained to find people buried in the ruins of buildings after an earthquake. In snowy mountains, they find people buried by avalanches. Many different types of dogs are used as sniffer dogs.

The world's best-trained dog

As the show ends, an agility contest takes place outside. The dogs have to complete an obstacle course – jumping hurdles, weaving between poles, going up and down stairs, and crawling through a tunnel. The winner is the dog that finishes fastest without making any mistakes.

Inheritance, experience, and training all play a part in agility contests.

Training matters

You watch the dogs run the course – they are amazing! Following their owner's shouts, whistles, and signals, they twist and turn to take the obstacles in the right order. As with the sniffer dogs, training has built on the dog's natural abilities and instincts.

Training pays off

The winner receives his prize. Wolfie is a crossbreed, an Alsatian-Greyhound cross. The dog combines the best qualities of both **breeds**. Greyhounds are very fast, while Alsatians are strong, clever, and easy to train. Breeders often cross two breeds to get a champion in classes such as agility contests, in which any dog can take part. Wolfie's name reflects his proud **ancestor**, the wolf!

Mixed-breed dogs

Dog shows are fun to watch, but **pedigree** or pure-breed dogs sometimes suffer from health problems. This is because breeders have only a small number of pedigree dogs to choose from if they want to breed a champion. Health problems, as well as good qualities, can be passed on in **genes**. Mixed-breed dogs (mongrels) are often healthier than pure-breed ones. They usually live longer. So a mixed breed is a great choice if you want a dog.

ancestor animal or person that an animal or person is descended from. The wolf is the ancestor of all domestic dogs.

breed small group within a species of animal

cell tiny unit that all living things are made out of

chromosome x-shaped structure found inside nucleus of a cell, which contains genes

DNA strings of chemicals inside cells that make up genes and form a code

domestic tame

dominant describes a gene that is strong and controls an inherited feature

fertilization moment when a male sex cell joins with a female egg, to start a new life

generation all the animals (or people) born and living at one time

genes sections of DNA that controls an inherited feature, such as eye or hair colour

gestation time between fertilization and birth, when a female animal is pregnant

heredity process through which features are passed on from parents to their young, also called inheritance

inheritance see heredity

mammal member of the group of animals with hair on their bodies, whose young feed on their mother's milk

mate when animals come together in order to have young

nucleus tiny dot at the centre of a cell, which controls how the cell works

offspring young of an animal

pedigree pure-bred animal that belongs to a recognized breed

recessive describes a gene that is weaker than a strong, or dominant, gene

selective breeding when a breeder chooses a particular animal to breed from because the animal has features that the breeder wants the offspring to have

species kind of living thing; members of a species can breed to make more members

sperm male sex cell

trait certain feature that an animal has

variation change or difference

womb space inside a female mammal in which the baby develops

Books

Dog (Eyewitness), Juliet Clutton-Brock (Dorling Kindersley, 2004)

Genes and DNA (Kingfisher Knowledge), Richard Walker (Kingfisher, 2003)

In Your Genes (Body Talk), Steve Parker (Raintree, 2007)

Inheritance and Reproduction (Essential Life Science), Jen Green (Heinemann Library, 2013)

The Usborne Introduction to Genes and DNA, Anna Claybourne (Usborne Publishing, 2003)

Websites

www.amnh.org/explore/ology/genetics
The website for the American Museum of Natural History has lots of information about genetics.

www.bbc.co.uk/schools/gcsebitesize/science/21c_pre_2011/genetics
This BBC Bitesize website has facts about genes and inheritance.

kidshealth.org/kid/talk/qa/what_is_gene.html
This website has simple explanation of genes and inheritance.

pbskids.org/dragonflytv/games/game_dogbreeding.html
Have fun with this genetics game. Try your hand breeding various types of Border Collie puppies.

www.sciencekidsathome.com/science_topics/genetics-a.html
There is another simple explanation of how genes work on this website.

Places to visit

The Science Museum
Exhibition Road
South Kensington
London
SW7 2DD
www.sciencemuseum.org.uk

Zoos are great places to find out more about animals. Find out about your nearest zoo at your library or on the internet.

Index

Afghan Hounds 6
African wildcats 14
agility contests 28–29
Alsatians (German Shepherds) 8, 29
ancestors 8
appearance 27

Basset Hounds 5
Beagles 20, 26
big cats 15
Bloodhounds 27
Border Collies 7
breeds 4, 7, 8, 9, 12, 14, 23, 29

canines 9
cats 14–16, 17, 19
cave paintings 9
cells 5, 11, 17, 18, 19, 21, 23
Chihuahuas 6, 7
chromosomes 17, 21, 23

Dachshunds 7
Dalmatians 4
DNA 17
dogs 4–11, 17, 19, 20, 21, 22–27
domestic animals 6, 8–9, 12, 14
dominant genes 25
draught horses 13

egg cells 18, 19, 21, 23, 25

Falabella ponies 13
fertilization 18, 19, 21
foals 19, 21

genes 5, 11, 15, 17, 19, 20, 22, 23, 25, 27, 29
gestation 19
Great Danes 7
Greyhounds 10–11, 29
gun dogs 7

hair colours 24–25
health problems 29
heredity see inheritance
horses and ponies 12–13, 15, 17, 21
hounds 7
humans 17, 19

inheritance 5, 11, 16, 21, 28
instincts 15, 29
Irish Wolfhounds 7

jackals 9

kittens 5, 19, 21

Labradors 7, 24, 25
litter sizes 19

Maine Coon cats 16
mammals 19, 21
Manx cats 14
Mastiffs 6, 7
mating 13, 19, 25
Mendel, Gregor 25
mixed-breed dogs 29
mongrels 29

natural abilities 9, 15, 26, 29
newborn mammals 21
nuclei 17

pedigree dogs 29
Persian cats 14
Pugs 6
puppies 5, 19, 21, 23
pure-breed dogs 29

recessive genes 25
reproduction 5, 18–19

Saint Bernards 6, 7
selective breeding 10, 13
sex cells 19, 21, 23
sex chromosomes 23
Siamese cats 14
Siberian Huskies 8
sniffer dogs 26, 27
species 6, 15
sperm 18, 19, 21, 23, 25
sports horses 13

"toy" dogs 7
training 26, 28, 29
traits 4, 5, 11, 17, 25

variations 22, 23

wild dogs 9
wolves 8, 9, 29
womb 19
working animals 7, 8–9, 12, 13, 26, 27